I0078832

SHEARSMAN

30

30TH ANNIVERSARY ISSUE

87 & 88

SPRING / SUMMER 2011

EDITED BY
TONY FRAZER

Shearsman magazine is published in the United Kingdom by
Shearsman Books Ltd
58 Velwell Road
Exeter EX4 4LD

www. shearsman.com

ISBN 978-1-84861-154-2
ISSN 0260-8049

This compilation copyright © 2011, Shearsman Books Ltd.
All rights in the works printed here revert to the authors, translators or original
copyright-holders after publication. Permissions requests may be directed to
Shearsman, but they will be forwarded to the copyright-holders.

Acknowledgements

The poems by Élise Turcotte translated here are from *Sombre ménagerie* (Eds. du
Noroît, Montreal, 2002), and appear by kind permission of the author and publisher.
'Recycling Starlight' by Penny Harter has appeared in an eponymous chapbook
(Mountains and Rivers Press, Eugene, OR), copyright Penny Harter, 2010.
Reprinted by permission of the author. The poems by Paol Keineg translated here
are drawn from *Triste Tristan* (Éditions Apogée, Rennes, 2004), and appear here
by permission of the author.

Subscriptions and single copies:

Current subscriptions—covering two double-issues, each around 108 pages, cost £13
in the UK, £16 for the rest of Europe (including the Republic of Ireland), and £18
for the rest of the world. Longer subscriptions may be had for a proportionately
higher payment, which insulates purchasers from further price-rises during the term
of the subscription.

Back issues from nº 63 onwards (uniform with this issue)—cost £8.50/$13.50
through trade channels. Single copies can be ordered for £8.50, post-free, direct
from the press, through the Shearsman online store, or from bookstores in the UK
and the USA. Earlier issues, from 1 to 62, may be had for £3 each direct from the
press, where they are still available, but contact us for prices for a full, or partial, run.

Submissions

Shearsman operates a submissions-window system, whereby submissions are only
considered during the months of March and September, at which point selections
are made for the October and April issues respectively. Submissions may be sent by
mail or email, but email attachments—other than PDFs—are not accepted. We aim
to respond within 2–3 months of the window's closure.

CONTENTS

CHRISTOPHER MIDDLETON

From the Grotto

Much blood spills in the kill and sharing out.
None smears our cave walls, as yet.

*

To make good I have spat, hoping for a bird
to take shape, a mouthful of manganese.

*

Here and now it will be forever home;
piqued by no phantoms we share and share alike.

*

A sight better than us, the beasts know
what is what. What if we made do with that?

*

We had luck and chose this shell of rock;
river glitters below, with fish we'll harpoon.

*

How temperate now these people are, they think
no gods could come and dare play dice with us.

*

I'll tell a story of how we came to be here.
Pleasure in the design will drive them to believe it.

An Archaic Greek Vase Painting

From left to right the long-legged
Triangular torsos, wasp-waisted
Figures step in time. On all four chins
Trim pointed beards can be discerned.

Black and white and on each side
Of the procession, small figures,
These too of men, had to be small: their stature
Allows for the curve of the vase
A potter projected his picture on.

*

Do they dance or are they carrying
Stiff on a board, dead but identical,
A male who is prone and turns his back on you?
He looks taller than his carriers.
Possibly they would be ephebes, and him—
Their modern champion, or Achilles.

*

Above the dead man there's a dense,
Ah, but before I get to that
I must mention the conspicuous letter M.
The letter M appears in spaces
Between the dancing carriers and around them,
As if to voice the whole town's moaning.
Some other little shapes are interspersed,
Baby helix, geometrical moth.

*

Now for the dense honeycomb of diagonals
Darkening the oblong above the corpse.
It is earth perhaps. Perhaps underneath
The dancers are not carrying him at all.
They lift their arms for the dancing;
They dance to honour a man entombed.

If he is entombed, the burial custom
Has been for the picture's sake modified,
He's lying not curled up or on his back,
But on his side, so that the harmonies
Of torso, hip, and calf-muscle, such as his,
Alive or dead, could always be admired.-

*

Eight tiny women, tiny because
Distanced by the upcurve of the clay,
Quite still they had to sit, above the honeycomb,
All facing to the right; lifted arms,
Palms laid flat on top of the head,
Copy the poise of the dancers underneath.

*

Between the women, white voids enclose,
Just look, with little rays shooting out,
Nine suns or stars, but they could represent
Just as well the seed of flowers in flight.

*

In black and white the scene spoke:
Polarity, a formal drama flesh acts out,
Gladdens or hurts. but harmony is constant.
Women and men, living and dead

Young and old model to their measure
Moments of night, moments of day;
As for their gods, who do not break faith
Piloting now and then people home at last,
Rites trim their mass but not their beauty.

Significantly less than seven inches tall
This formal scene, a glimpse. Taken off-guard
We know that what we know will not be all.

A True Tale of the Anecdotes Improvised by Villiers de L'Isle-Adam

Ropes in their coils now the men have cast off
And the Mariner eyes the deep—
So in a bar that is gaslit
And homely to him, though it reeks of piss,
Villiers would begin, impromptu, an anecdote.

Marvels he spoke, and the air burned them up.
Marvels, we say, for they were not bookish.
To this day the bright legend travels by voice.

But when invited to collect between covers
Some of his stories, Villiers
Could barely account for those he had published.

As the Mariner puts in at a hospitable island
For supplies of water and meat,
So Villiers knocked on the door of the Master.

Welcomed in, Villiers watches the silent
Master withdraw into a room apart.

Soon the Master is stepping forth with an Album:
Saved from the daily papers and reviews,
All the stories Villiers could not account for.
The Master had harvested every tale in print.

Of the impromptus not a scrap
Came down to us. All went up in smoke—
Gone with the old Parisian reek of piss.

True, their *fraîcheur* had to fascinate as much
As anything Villiers wrote on paper:
And now even more so—

        As long as the anecdotes,
Richly flowing, leaped toward horizons of hasard,
Make-do phrasing likely
Tempered the thrust of recital; but
As the legend about them prospered, those anecdotes,
Not in the least bookish, lit all the faces up.

Even in ink, unbookish tales
Such as were spoken in gaslight once
Might be no mirage: Eldorados for feeling,
Not even the ghost of a statement in them;
life-giving their book of mysterious vagaries,
like space the Mariner houses in his compass,
Evolves to measure and in perspective.

Rosmarie Waldrop

War, You Write

for Esther Tellermann

And: in the beginning was death, black black behind the eyes, the light from below, the waters ungathered.

Whether in war or peace, we carry our bones wherever we go. Counting how foot follows foot on the ground; and idea, idea in the mind. Or not. The air does not resist. Thus it refutes us.

How plant the roots we come from, you write, artifice, effort, fatigue, the image subsumed, sifting to settle, approach the river, the troops at the ready.

Trapped in the skull, a roar we cannot recognize. In terms of "the nature of war." Or repair in parallel sentences, with punctuation in the right places. Rain, storms, fire from all sides. But the best way to measure time, says St. Augustine, is by reading a poem.

Our war was mental, you write, a net toward the insides of skirmish, raid, raw pronoun, preposition in ambush, patrol, pitched battle.

Even if the clock stops, each cell pulses. Deep in the body we feel silently flowing water. Consciousness plays its searchlight on this image and on the surface of this image. The flesh turns transparent, and the organs sit next to one another. We refine our ability to kill.

Thirst was the inherent cause, you write, shared language of destruction, mutilation, waxy days, the tribe of warriors rode down the abstractions.

Not far below the skin, the habit of pillage, rape, murder, flash of fire along our arms. Compatible with gestures in vain from a clean, well-lighted street. The physicist sees the passage of time as loss of organization. But the rhythm of a sentence, like the water we drink from the faucet, has the form of our inner sense. And one minute devours the next.

The poem is ashes, you write, set free on the inner surface of the world. Thus it remembers.

RAY DiPALMA

The Persistence of Memory

> Very evil people cannot really be imagined dying.
> —Adorno

The wall against which they
flattened their backs and raised their arms
without quite knowing themselves—
some former pedestrians some former individuals

sacrificed to a perpetuation
of the modes of indifference
approval and dissolution

talking through broken doors
fatal witnesses to apocryphal knowledge
that harbored the means of the ancient wound

propaganda and admonition
ensured a turning point—merely
a transference of loss to reflex-dominated pathos
abandoned to the calamitously relative

Site

Buried today
No, buried yesterday

The light rain had stopped
The late May evenings still cool

Lapsus in ms. but not in substance
The light rain diswritten discomposed

Thought to sit through—the floor turning
You are found composed of last lines

The floor turning thought
You are found

A fragile alignment will get this back

Nostalgia remembers how to seem

The vertical bars placed closer together
The horizontal arranged further apart

An Expense of Blue Pigment

Attentive to the unquestioned finality
the esteem that exults in its rags

I went to sleep wondering
and nothing is more difficult

a triple consequence of all that
had happened only hours before

vanishing causes whose powers are
surprising because they conceal themselves in logic

inconceivable to reason while still remaining legible
accorded not closure but a closed subject

whose sole pretext curiosity alone remains assailable
no more than a name that was sought barely a word

forewarned though I was I must have tried to explain
only to find myself both understood and inexplicable

Pictures at an Excavation

                                    The sun is wrong—
as if it was only now—as if when was finished
though still facing both ways—when alone in the shade
of these scattered unwanted remains—
must have got a cramp no one heard the shouts they could say—
never what they think never what they know only what they suspect

Disgust is consequence in the service of repetition
getting it all down while casting aside the pell mell and aging
for emphasis for analysis all very corrective
all very lifelike it deeply engages attribution without remorse
coded UPON DELIVERY declared late and poorly
"Thus" being spoken after the fork in the road is taken—
bleak with detail and dread familiar themes
the air thinner here at the front of the line—so many

SUSAN CONNOLLY

The Sun Artist

at the Cross of Muiredach, Monasterboice, c. 850–2009AD

```
              d e e p s h a d o w e d
    s     d e e p s h a d o w e     s
      s     d e e p s h a d o w     s
    s u       d e e p s h a d o     s u
    s u       d e e p s h a d     s u
    s u n       d e e p s h a     s u n
    s u n       d e e p s h     s u n
    s u n s       d e e p s     s u n s
    s u n s       d e e p     s u n s
    s u n s e       d e e     s u n s e
    s u n s e       d e     s u n s e
    s u n s e t       d     s u n s e t
      s u n s e t       s u n s e t
    s u n s e t       r     s u n s e t
    s u n s e t       r e     s u n s e t
    s u n s e       r e n     s u n s e
    s u n s e       r e n e     s u n s e
    s u n s       r e n e w     s u n s
    s u n s       r e n e w s       s u n s
    s u n       r e n e w s r       s u n
    s u n       r e n e w s r e       s u n
    s u       r e n e w s r e n       s u
    s u       r e n e w s r e n e       s u
      s       r e n e w s r e n e w       s
    s       r e n e w s r e n e w s       s
    f       r e n e w s r e n e w s       f
    f       r e n e w s r e n e w       f
    f a       r e n e w s r e n e       f a
    f a       r e n e w s r e n       f a
    f a d       r e n e w s r e       f a d
    f a d       r e n e w s r       f a d
    f a d i       r e n e w s       f a d i
    f a d i       r e n e w       f a d i
    f a d i n       r e n e       f a d i n
    f a d i n       r e n       f a d i n
    f a d i n g       r e       f a d i n g
    f a d i n g       r       f a d i n g
    f a d i n g       f a d i n g
      f a d i n       p       f a d i n
    f a d i n       p a       f a d i n
      f a d i       p a t       f a d i
    f a d i       p a t t       f a d i
      f a d       p a t t e       f a d
    f a d       p a t t e r       f a d
      f a       p a t t e r n       f a
    f a       p a t t e r n s       f a
      f       p a t t e r n s p       f
    f       p a t t e r n s p a       f
        p a t t e r n s p a t
```

deepshadowed sunset renews fading patterns

```
        i l l u m i n a t i o n
  s       i l l u m i n a t i o       s
  s       i l l u m i n a t i         s
  s u     i l l u m i n a t       s u
  s u     i l l u m i n a         s u
  s u d   i l l u m i n         s u d
  s u d   i l l u m i           s u d
  s u d d i l l u m           s u d d
  s u d d i l l u             s u d d
  s u d d e i l l             s u d d e
  s u d d e i l               s u d d e
  s u d d e n i               s u d d e n
  s u d d e n       s u d d e n
  s u d d e n s     s u d d e n
  s u d d e n s h   s u d d e n
  s u d d e s h a   s u d d e
  s u d d e s h a d s u d d e
  s u d d s h a d o s u d d
  s u d d s h a d o w s u d d
  s u d s h a d o w s s u d
  s u d s h a d o w s h s u d
  s u s h a d o w s h a s u
  s u s h a d o w s h a d s u
  s s h a d o w s h a d o s
  s s h a d o w s h a d o w s
  w s h a d o w s h a d o w w
  w s h a d o w s h a d o w
  w o s h a d o w s h a d w o
  w o s h a d o w s h a w o
  w o r s h a d o w s h w o r
  w o r s h a d o w s w o r
  w o r l s h a d o w w o r l
  w o r l s h a d o w o r l
  w o r l d s h a d w o r l d
  w o r l d s h a w o r l d
  w o r l d s s h w o r l d s
  w o r l d s s w o r l d s
  w o r l d s w o r l d s
  w o r l d f w o r l d
  w o r l d f l w o r l d
  w o r l f l u w o r l
  w o r l f l u t w o r l
  w o r f l u t t w o r
  w o r f l u t t e w o r
  w o f l u t t e r w o
  w o f l u t t e r i w o
  w f l u t t e r i n w
  w f l u t t e r i n g w
```

sudden   illumination   shadow-worlds   fluttering

One Hundred and Six Days

For Sharon Commins, Ireland, and Hilda Kawuki, Uganda, aid workers,
abducted and held hostage for over three months in North Darfur, Sudan

```
        a   i   d   w   o   r   k   e   r   s
    a                                           r
        c   o   m   m   i   n   s
    b     c   o   m   m   i   n
            c   o   m   m   i
    d         c   o   m   m               l
            c   o   m
    u     x         c   o           x     e
        x   x           c           x   x
    c     x                           x   a
                    d   i
    t             n   s   r                 s
                a   s   h   a   e
    e         l   s   h   a   r   o   l       e
            e   s   h   a   r   o   n   s   a
    d   r   s   h   a   r   o   n   s   h   a   n   d
    i   s   h   a   r   o   n   s   h   a   r   o   d
        s   h   a   r   o   n   s   s   h   a   r   o   n
    u   s   h   a   r   o   n   s   h   a   r   o   a
        g   s   h   a   r   o   n   s   h   a   d
            a   s   h   a   r   o   n   s   n       o
                n   s   h   a   r   o   a
    j           d   s   h   a   g           c
                a   s   u
    u     x                       x       t
        x   x       r   d       x   x
    l     x       u   h   a       x       o
            f   h   i   l   r
    y           r   h   i   l   d   a   f       b
            a   h   i   l   d   a   h   i   u
        d   h   i   l   d   a   h   i   l   d   r   e
        h   i   l   d   a   h   h   i   l   d   a
    s   h   i   l   d   a   h   i   l   d   n   r
        u   h   i   l   d   a   h   i   a
            d   h   i   l   d   a   d
                a   h   i   l   u
                n   h   s
            x                       x
    2   x   x           k           x   x   2
            x       k   a           x
    0           k   a   w               0
            k   a   w   u
    0       k   a   w   u   k           0
            k   a   w   u   k   i
    9                                       9
        h   o   s   t   a   g   e   s
```

Laundry and Wonder
for GG

> Drugs in garland
> edge her gangways

Gala lewd, dyed and lunged

> An aged waggery null, wrung

A ragged ally with (equally) ragged lungs

> She yawns and dangles, raw
> She glares like an August lawn
> Gulls and gully danger her gardens

> Rage and gnawed, grayed

The walled gulag laden in alder
> in lawyer glad

> An unwary runaway: she is gluey
> > wary
> > wan

Her grand drag unwell
aged like drywall
> like (mathematics)

Eggs in error put in with the laundry: gangs of angels in
their larded waggle

> The Lady yawns legalisms
> her gear argyle: a dawn in rags

Laundry Ugly
An allergy regally, waggery, grange

Really!

Rude duels, naggery

The wall or war: a gray lawn
The lawn gulled with yarn, drawn in her warn(ings)

Fear of Hotels and Photography
after a dream by Diane Arbus (1959)

Pressed with want
in an enormous flowered hotel
She is condemned to fire
The building contains both stopping and wandering
Quiet and idle in golden elevators

A white hotel filled with a morning on fire
in the form of enormous blossoms
I am pressed to the I extremely
My grandmother is perhaps under this room
How the building divides her
How much time in canned food, photography?
Perhaps she is not really in this movie
We are seized and strolled by neighbors
peaceful and idle in golden elevators

In the white hotel, there is only one morning left inside
condemned to fire in enormous blooms
Smoke hangs in proximity, particularly in light somewhat

I am operated by photography and I extremely
How much preserved food? How much photography?
How long is the self?
Seized and sauntered in neighborhoods
calm and dormant in these golden elevators

>There is an enormous flower where the hotel
>was criticized by fire
>An allotment of morning in white
>But the burning marks calmly form a person
>an I in order to suck in tobacco, nearness
>The light cannot consider fire everywhere
>I operate, become photographic, set-up, very
>If I, then building divides me
>The food, the photographic set-up
>where I maintained myself long on my own
>Perhaps there is no film left in me
>The I stop frequently, everyone gasps, saunters
>As for the dormant calm, neighbors
>in their gold elevators

Enormous criticism and the tickets burn inside morning
A person in thin allotment
Light where it will swell up inside order
She is dog tobacco sucking up fact, nearness to spare
That does purity quite
Probably this photograph discovers the hazards
inside a camera
Seized and sauntered, in gold

>Criticized in this non-place
>in a non-fevered morning
>In the white hotel quite, slowly, willfully, in
>constant matter

A person in thin allotment
The I dog, tobaccoed, sucked inside order
To forgive near fact
Her photographed hypotheses quite
systematic when the I is deposited inside an
        exact region
I order the I inside skin, and it arrives
I will divide the building and search for food to
        photograph
The camera is dangerous and systematic
film saunters in gold

The map of the place is criticized as not the place at all
not in morning enormously
Fevered in a white hotel
a flower in constant temperature
The light stops in letters, absorption
tobacco sucked like a fact

Her acceptance of control changes the
        photograph completely
Skin in order to arrive
He goes longitudinally for food
at the end of manufacture
An orderly examination of time
The person and the situation, a constant
        temperature
The proximity that apprehends everything
laundered in gold

To map this place enormously
not the fever of mornings
An intentional affair in thin dispatch
She sucks the tobacco out of order

out of forgiveness to pursue form
That only quite
Photography and hypothesis hand has quite
If the I does not lay down and order itself in skins
probably the morning will lay down, sauntered

> We are programmed by place enormously
> and the inner parts of our fevers
> Transaction intentionally enters the hotel
> To send in thin light, writing swells in
> absorption
> A pardoned fact close to the shape it pursues
> The skins order the I, the I divides under
> construction
> eliminated in moreover
> The I eliminated through food
> The film is in order not inner
> gripped by vicinity, we are sauntered in gold

If not reproached by force
we find a map of too much place
That no mornings ever had a fever
nevertheless this I is deliberate
in the constant bloom of temperature
Affairs walk through the white hotel in thin missions
Expert in certain forgiveness
and the narrow forms you follow
This Only is enough

> The hands of our affairs, systemic, in ordered I,
> skin regions
> If I divide the building, it proves you are not
> essential
> Photograph foods manufactured by force

I long for the mine that knew
Probably that him you discover
that dangerous machine, that systemic you in film
The person and the situation, in neighborhoods
lifted in occupied golden

* * *

An impatient pleasure
not be confused with photography
Kinder in calms
The employees ask you to be held from behind
because they are not ready
Surmounted by pleasure
infested with his interruptions
Cupids cut him out of the ceiling
They continue to disappear from the film

Likely drops in strength incomparably
She is filled with a double-featured fun
Defeated in morning by a severed pleasure, he
        to harass
Has Cupid obliterated the ceiling?
She thinks "preserve and vanish"
neglect worried into their fear
Urgent in slow and attach

Largely incomparable
improbable drops in strength
An impatient river does not run in order to be photographed
The calm stops painfully, the morning separates pasts
by the pleasure of him to press, covered in, wiped out
"Wipe that love off your feet before you come in"

They continue disappearing, as indicated by all possible marks
But I provide myself
in order to neglect their fear for me
in slow motion probable

       I: a sufficiency of characteristic recreation
       to be impatiently rivered
       The calms stop painfully
       I am almost demolished as the morning separates
       beyond a tightening pleasure
       Under cover to eliminate love

Forced falls mainly incomparable, probable
Impatience does not join the river in calm interims
The mornings separate close to pleasure
as if the I were to preserve anything
The camera continues to disappear
no one indicated in the possible marks
The I supplies itself
In the end neglect fears me
in morning, urgent eyed

       An inimitableness in defeated hope
       failing mainly
       the I is a sufficiently unique recreation
       Impatience in the river's edges
       The calm intervals of pain felt and stopped
       As for me, almost demolishes
       Morning, the joy of closing, compression divided
       She tore off the cover from the book of love

Hope falls mainly in an inimitable defeat
in the singular recovery of sufficiency
The edge of a river, or photography

an overwhelming form of control
The calm distances the pain of the thing
But morning the joy in reasoning
that the other side of compression is divided
Love, with its cover removed
Possibly if I, because it is close to photography
Curiosity continues to expire
compiled and urgent in slow movement

       In She: a reestablished sufficiency

An impatient end to him
by the river, in a photograph
neutralizing types
Reason compacted into a form of reasoning
Probably she is in terms of curiosity
All likely clues but himself
The elasticity of "so"
Need credited outdoors:
a form for which she adopts a syntax
in slow locomotion

           This him extremely impatient
           in regard to any uniqueness
           past arriving
           The calm intervals of pain
           neutralized by preparation
           You can divide the packing
           his demolished pliability
           how morning interferes with joy

The camera for the thing that cannot
The photographic I thing you understand
The confidence spared outside fear of the necessity of the thing

Elasticity, on the shoals of form
Meeting where she supposes syntax out of these edges
something offers itself, extracted from direction
Slow movements related to inferior mornings

      In hope of defeat, inimitable
      Calm distances, pliability demolished
      Love extracted from morning joys
      Fording the elasticity, an assumed syntax
      wrung out

Ekphrasis

These Mozambican figures
in the billionaire's African Collection,
phantasmagoric. One of a spirit
standing on a man's bent back
and hacking into his spine, though the grimace
such he could have been eating flesh,
drinking from a skull-cup. Like the protean
in Mia Couto's tales: war's phenomenology,
how photos 'capture' what we either struggle
to remember or can't forget, our regressing
to the scene of the crime
as to a lost country, edenic.

Coimbra

Slitting open the pages of an edition
of *The Tragedy of Inês de Castro,*
reflecting on the experimental
poets of Coimbra, their insistence
on the dissolution of the FIRST PERSON,
you remember, earlier in the day,
picking oranges for the first time
in your life, floating, a cosmonaut,
between the suns in an Australian's
poem, and then, somehow anticipating Inês,
THE FIGURE, you must have read elsewhere,
as effigy, as corpse, you are wondering
whether your own dissolution has begun,
whether, between these memories,
you were SELF, or could be 'mere'
allusion, a cloud, drifting;

Question for António Damásio

Doesn't all European thought
disappear into the Void
between Spinoza and Pessoa,
that cornucopia
of nerves and that Tibetan
skull-cup?

This Era
—*for Goenawan Mohamad*

      Philosophical as always,
the Indonesian poet's essay
      on the Indian Ocean Tsunami
as the Lisbon Earthquake of our day,

      questions, not quite as Voltaire did,
the Future that always follows disaster,
      that wakefulness
after each, *Inshallah!*

Stalking Gerald Manley Hopkins

I've been reading your diary and sniffing its flowerbeds
The white violets are broader and smell of *April 15, 1871*
treading in my bare reader's feet the sharper whelking and
a more winged recoil in the leaves. I've left some of the days
to themselves, unfinished like Spring, 1871, April 21
We have had other such afternoons, one today—the sky a

I've whisked past that specific (it was *beautiful grained*) blue
and backwards to peruse you, in letters to your father,
to read you caught believing, between him *16 October 1866*
You are so kind as not to forbid me your house, to which I have no claim,
on condition, if I understand, that I promise not to try to convert
my brothers and sisters

and your superiors   Before I can promise this I must get permission,
wh. I have no doubt will be given. Of course this promise
will not apply after they come of age. Closeness to a God penning
the distance—grown child's to parent's soul—that's as much
like doubt as faith *Whether after my reception you will still speak*
as you do now I cannot tell

I can spell no comfort in my witness's wince, though I spy onwards
irreverent with chronology and plundering half-sprung authorship,
          poet
to his pal *15 Feb 1879   When I say that I do not mean to publish*
I speak the truth. I can wedge myself in between you, your mum and
Marvel *most rich and nervous* of verse, not knowing who I was
looking for in your bud-filled universe until via post-Herbert Vaughan
27 Feb 1879 . . . and even his muse underwent a conversion
(for he had written before).

Arranged Marriage

'Ladies and Gentlemen, please be
upstanding for the Bride and Groom'
Wedding toast, Master of Ceremonies.

The body remembers
its down on all fours
by fridge. How the distance
from phone in next room
was travelled, a blank. In
any case, by fridge
chest-clench as muscles of
all parts tried to take
in the new
s a non-digestion: agony
become gesture: animal
howl-less, lips clamped
shut for the days that
followed, unsolitary
in their weeks.

Months later, the body
lets me forget that
it remembers, knows
the same position is
used for birth, that it
wonders
if I place knee and knee
and both palms down, on
cold floor would I return
and be closer to you
leaving? The answer
that it breathes, in
an exhale still—

still suspended from
that December chest:
you would, perhaps, expire.

Were you to assume that
position, lung and lung
and heart would either
cease or fire. So, this up-
right prayer to limb and head:
forget the harm. Please,
please remain standing—

A Language

The accident of speaking one's
mind, like traffic accident or child
and erring bowel. Sewn to the fault
lines once said, related beings scatter
in a savaged knowing, seismic shift.

The chanced truths of human eye: contact
crazily loud, if read in bed or park or
repro room. Glanced out, up to light from
soul's soil, cut flower to be found in gut
-ter by stranger language looking.

Loving, the logos to be found
in all that causes such primal
vowel moan, vibrations sound.

The Writer's Portrait

Sun beats that bashful brain
protectionless and exposing
itself as if to pervert, to off-
er alteration from an original
course, meaning or state to
a distortion. Corruption of
what was, first intended,
natural? The abnormality
and sex ever-present, thump
as solar power. Pulse.

by a haunting

what I mean is the of course of [rain]
listening to slow harm
as   (is this the town or the country
you decide)
                    chimneys fresh outmoded
gas-lit perhaps   a miracle's atmosphere
filmed sheen as paths cross

I could have remembered you into this
but it's already too complicated
contemplation eased over
diluted songs undermining a certain flavour
concentrated repression behind closed eyes

you become the moment before a calm starts
widowing   widening out   grief movements

to believe is to have come a long way
[mist] circling   a kept thing losing time
to stop   when   it all becomes too beautiful

details of the impending season

it is no longer necessary to look for

instead things are   waiting
shadowed shadows inside your head

weighted glottal stops the shape of angina
see where your eyes were

porcelain bulbs
gone out for the night tracing a last bus in september

rain is where we fall failing to form

at least there is an hour before   [~~looking forgets you~~]
sunrise makes its arrests   allowed as far
wombs to divert to

later we'll set out

it seems again the open door fits in

brush me gently and I will speak you
for what it matters
                              means to

elegant society pearl bright in your mirrors
a stern stiff lampshade melting with century dew

another option conceals the first
as cars colliding on a motorway fist tomorrows

where I know you were alive when the bridge left
above certain things that weren't important before

GARETH DURASOW

Regina Lisso

The little box, instrument of metaphysical shrinkage, wasn't intended to witness the intrusion of ultimate realities.
        —*Eugenia Parry*

        Lee Miller at Leipzig
the statue that came to life in the Blood of a Poet
photographs the selbstmord in the Rathaus
        Mors certa, hora incerta
the parents just bodies but the daughter Regina
chiaroscuro courtesy of the hour
        Regina you have such Fabergé teeth
the very pietà the Third Reich deserves
coiffure dishevelled by furtive caresses
gaunt young men compelled to touch your will-o-the-wisp hair
        Permission to sit with her awhile
to defibrillate her with my eyes
a kiss so voltaic
her needlepoint hands unfurl &
Vogue all over my roughshod face
        Nurse's fingers gone to waste
expending their vestiges of dexterity
unpicking a button from the upholstery
like a girl chastised in the fairy wing repair shop
plucks out an offensive eye
        To sleep more soundly in the sun's black spot
a Rammstein espresso shot straight down her throat
                derailing all the enzymes till the air is no use.

Preludes

1.

a Cold War bench mosquitoes & Coolidge
the poetry mother warned you about
a fresh of breath air & (without
limitation) the sky is an exit wound
octopus blart in a grey cornea
Bob Hoskins' face
at the end of The Long Good Friday
in other words look how much is going on in there

2.

that theirs was the conscience round one could ascertain from the kick
but the burning man is not a samizdat
the hanging man no fruit
better a bullet breach the cardiac
muscle thru the hip-
flask of Private Eddie Slovik
back against the wall
condemned for the brass he stole when he was just a kid

3.

trampled under a white Xmas we bow our heads
to totems less abstract than a porcelain Christ
this one is lightly oaked adding a little extra body
& subtle hints of spice
pay ringside prices to stone mistaken
weathermen dead. Confederate troops
arrayed in ranks of moderate rock
to build McDonalds from the blood clot up

Romancero

Incredibly—from vertical to horizontal in one
moment (moment as long as some sang pas-
sages in bygone eras from a named purgatory
to their named heaven) the day, turning from
tempest to just fine; all lowering clouds drowning
the earth to smiling azures; brown landscape
turned to green; the silent birds now perpetrating
riots of conjugated melody. Romantic time has,
true, evolved from patience to consumption. Be-
low the birthplace of the earth is seen, wreathed
in black, blond and burnished auras – its mines
await the miner while from blood and lymph he
turns mud into gold and diamonds. Higher than
centrifugal valley all senses radiating, the birth-
place puckered symbol smiling in its heartland,
twin mountains holding up the planet high above
the centripetal turtle understanding. Higher yet,
those two-way windows giving/receiving, opening
wide onto the widest azure sky, closing as breath
comes faster, as flights of fancy multiply and mas-
tery of life flowers and spreads its seeds with wind-
like laughter. Is it not passing brave to be a king
and ride in triumph through Persepolis? But now,
however, the novel's on its downward path—it
must decline into misunderstanding or ghastly tra-
gedy and winds dissolve to tears. To lamentations.
Readers, dreading the end, yet racing to the end –
as if another death were to be added to a list, a li-
tany of deaths, begin to try to think, prod memory
for last reviewer's commendations; the choices of
the famous for the year's best produce (*famosi* ah!),
to court desire, to count and to make notes of which-

soever other plots, why, just might satisfy: but, what,
by *other* authors than this present one? No, god for-
bid, this tittle-tattler by far a favorite, one cannot
exit from his list, plots, famous / infamous, his grand
finales so vastly credible no other maker to whom
one can subscribe lives now on earth, publishes day-
ly, reads to a vast, adoring public on 365 out of 365:
despite book-perishing, publishes on, endures forever.
This is no fair description of the greatest writer. Now
rage devours his reader's mind; great dragons of de-
sire break, overwhelm his will. Black clouds are back,
depressing him into the garden. Oh for Persepolis!

The Houses

The houses on the cliff can block the bay,
thought it is still there
      between them and in memory.
Ocean like
in flatness and dark amoebic shadows
      of weed on this calm day,
our anger's only periodic,
just when the four-master's passing,
seen only in blinks
      in the interstices,
but the houses have no volition.

Anger at objects, as if people's
      mistakes and miscreant behaviors,
fighting off the passage of time's
perpetuality, the body's noted accelerants,
as we grow older...
      the frozen bolt rusted,
a chain-saw that won't start.

"Come to me now in your sure fading,
put your foot on my neck,
before twisting me.
Sentimental,
      I too was born from the dead
conventionally,
but that was years ago."

This, then, is the dream that rises
like a whale in that calm water
glimpsed only in the interstices,
      those fucking houses
blocking our view.

Twisted

The short dog strains against the leash.
He wants that bone
          in the traffic and its flesh too,
a leg left behind;
skid marks, and a black shoe
at the temporary barricade.

Vinnie's energized by hit and run
and a chemical adrenalin,
that nun
          limping at the mission steps
on crutches.
He's in a Buick this time,
                    wide enough for narrow streets,
and California flowers, bloody as his fender,
spill at the curbs.

Her prayers rise
like chicken feathers in the wind:
          O patron saint of missing limbs,
avocados and beach party bingo.
Sister Carolyn
          Medina's lost her passion
for Christ and pastoral charity.
It's shampoo
for the short dog and a butcher's bone,
perfunctory novenas for her nemesis.

I was idling at the corner
watching the low-rider, in deference
          to the Sisters of Mercy.
Let these apparitions pass in the crosswalk.
I was free of all attachments,
though an orthopedic surgeon and the donor.

A golden chalice on the seat beside Vinnie,
Christ's picture
        on a deck of holy cards,
a bag full of cheap scapulas and rosaries,
                those earth laden roots
at his shoulder.
Theft planned to appear indiscriminate
after their rendezvous
in the garden near the parish sacristy.

I was there for the tree planting
        ceremony at the mission's new wing:
a sister, with a shovel
            at her black hem;
and photographers, newspaper writers, parishioners
represented by the chosen one,
        whose skirts rose easily for father McGonigle.
Not sister Carolyn Medina, not soon enough.
The one she'd thought of as her friend in Christ.

She came coyly forward on her crutches
        in habit and impossible dream.
At least I was fingering my rosary.
A bacchanal
among artificial limbs and braces, scent
        of flesh along some inner thigh
so virginal in California traffic.

She'd lifted her foot to the shovel,
in dignified posture in rain.
Vision of her name then
        on the tree's replacement,
ceremony for a brass plaque: *Sister Carolyn
        Medina Commemorates The Loss . . . ,*
but it was that fair-weather friend once again
and I was the donor of the plaque too.

What they called beach party bingo,
        eating avocados on the blanket at Laguna,
anonymous
among the recently rich and hip.
He was Sean again
        in his early sixties, high energy
from celibacy:
old man open to a younger woman
                with intentions, groaning,
more self-directed than he.

How mysterious, when I autoclaved the chicken,
the short dog perched upon her lap
                and Vinnie at the surgical table
in cast shadows,
        fiddling with the stirrups and the leash.
One remembers such nights only
as infra-slim,
        that space between earthy roots
                and oil of yesterday on artificial limbs,
our abstinence of chicken skin;
breath of dark interior virginal in air.

Father McGonigle wrote plans for the nemesis
and received some in return.
        He's in a California city, drives a car
and has civilian clothes.
Yet he can't find the proper
        surplice, his holy pictures, and the old
tarnished chalice
just won't do.

He thinks he'll call the authorities,
then he sees Sister
Carolyn Medina at the window and remembers

                the posture of his nemesis
among leaves,
                        now a vacancy, in rain
at the mission's new wing.
He's standing there,
throbbing for an understanding.

Vinnie's in a Chrysler this time, the nemesis
name cut in brass on the seat beside him
and spoils of the sacristy,
a surplice and impetuous letters.
                Sisters of Holy Mother Church
are in the crosswalk,
and the short dog's barking for his bone.

Then Sister Carolyn Medina's limping
                at the mission steps,
heading for candles and forgiveness
in perfunctory novenas.
                        A shade shifts at the window.
I await those artificial limbs in my office,
                and Vinnie's wrapped in his bloody fenders,
cruising the twisted
streets of Los Angeles.

Four Untitled Poems

"You are the hottest one for years of night . . ."

John Berryman wrote, in #4 of *The Dream Songs*, about
a keenly desired woman eating chicken nearby for whom he

(if I make the error of calling the poem's narrator
the poet himself) hungers. But when he reads it aloud he says,

"You are the hottest one for days of night . . ."

I prefer years. Listening to the recording it's obvious
he often reads different words from what's

in print. Wishing he'd written something else? Or
careless with his own writing, disdaining the bridges

of words he'd built, not wishing to cross
silence the same way again? Or wanting to sing and dream

a little differently each time? Needing
to be free of all that's boring, especially himself?

§

Lorine Niedecker's Good Success Bay
in her poem 'Darwin'—now there

in a poem of glaciers and pigeons, barnacles
and delirium, Port Desire and Andean Peaks

Darwin ravenous for the sound of the pianoforte
there

books
are slow work

the indigo
sea

out the window

§

nuns fishing on wharves chaos of clouds above habits

§

the older couple on their first date
behind us in the restaurant
have both talked about -exes and now agree
they like John
Travolta in everything
he's done

Epigrams of Summer

> 'as a haunted man—a man haunted
> with a memory—he was harmless'
> Henry James, *The Wings of the Dove*

Two coots have built their nest
on a tipped-over shopping trolley;
a mattress of wet plastic litter
supports the twigs they meshed together.

Now mother coot is sitting pretty
in shallows and her found-art splendour,
while, me, I find a theme from whatever
happens to be happening . . .

*

Bedraggled summer, overblown,
comes at us from under trees,
their thick-surging leafage
near summer's full opacity.

So you see this opaque world
(its piled clouds once more making
a three-dimensional sky)
carries us on its broad shoulders.

*

Walking back into that world once known,
there are glints of copper pipe-work,
fuss and palaver in pointed brick,
privet hedges, you alone . . .

Then a piffling kerfuffle of weather
might blear the window pane
with your memories of judgment,
of being judged again.

*

Sensitive to initial conditions,
here I am back in a Britain
like memories of things written,
the white roots under turned stones;

and find I'm living a broken series
of acronyms, every new-to-me term,
rain scents, words or idiom—
things to get done beyond these.

*

It's like we've got to do to others
what had been done to me
and there's no help in it, you say,
for that misery—

as if I could be both quick and dead
by lapping river water, a
world once known, bankrupted,
etcetera, etcetera . . .

*

Cow-parsley, buttercups, seed-heads
in extents of moving waves

are traipsed past by late revellers,
the house-backs like a stain.

Late revellers in their dribs-and-drabs
come murmuring out of the dawn.
Overcast, a morning greets them,
and what remains of their lives.

*

It's a Sunday, long before car noise,
and youth's in this June daylight:
one carries a girlfriend on his back;
others stalk with naked feet

from summers gone, at other dawns,
cloudless skies, bird choruses,
a yard's tree shadow thrown against
its house-back like a stain.

*

Momentary, come bungalows,
anemone-filled gardens, and enemy
infiltrations—
as if these were the front line . . .
Far fields are flecked with poppies.
It's like a mute complaint
about the further sacrifices,
this compliant scene!

*

Invisible beyond a taxi's windscreen,
pasts blank me, on the High Street,
like none of it had ever been
over grounds where we can't meet.

Just so, the pasts won't speak,
except in sly objection—
money, lust or interest,
most other values gone.

*

My projections of irrational fears
on cornered, desperate men
are summoned in the summer losses,
a village's mourning routine

or like an attack on the everyday
at Hungerford and Dunblane
or Whitehaven, us, implicated
in lives not being enough again.

*

Yet still things come and steady you
at a pumping house arched window,
its biscuit-brickwork textures
a survivor down the years.

My hand remembers what it would do
to get through tricky transitions,
pinching between forefinger and thumb
that scrap of shirtiness too.

*

From traffic by Christ's Pieces
those pasts can still be caught
in my heart-rate, chest,
lawns where we tried goodbyes . . .

Reflected in the river's flow
now other pairs are drifting past
under a guestroom window,
towards this Bridge of Sighs—

*

as elsewhere, they've renewed
a path across the grounds;
dusty, bereft of lampposts,
the old paths trouble knows.

Even water birds foul this new one.
Beyond a weariness and fret,
another life's to be retrieved
under the leaves of summer.

*

But here, I walk back under leaves
past black wrought-iron gates,
over flagstones sunk in grass
and more checkered shades.

Through the event-filled ordinary
postponements of that life,
these ghosts, you might suppose,
had our pasts in sole possession.

*

Like attacks on the everyday
or kind of self-betrayal,
how could they not spoil
this summery array?

Then come the extra mile
to exorcise those years,
a dazzle of sunshine appears
and words, words to say.

*

In ill-lit rooms across town
lives had altered course;
their ghosts on a horizon
(it's understood between us)

are dazzled by the mote-stream
as currents of talk along backs
come clearer in fresh air
and lift them away.

MARTIN ANDERSON

The Banana Archive

"My children too have learned a barbarous tongue".
Tu Fu.

I

Alone in this dead city by the salt marsh. City I long to leave. City I long to return to. Each morning workers coughing on their way to the factory. Each evening mist over the quiet quays. After the export trade declined. Importers now of oil and wood, of electronics and food. After the sea withdrew its bounty from us. Exporters of spent uranium and industrial waste. Poisonous rains at twilight. The river with its dead dogs. Two blocks away the Mint, the Ministry of Financial Services. Close by, the Numismatic Museum. Behind dressed granite generation after generation of the country's Kings and Queens, Emperors and Empresses, pseudo Sultans and Satraps: their heads embossed in gold. From far flung corners of the globe. A collective effulgence. Now, in the gloom of yet another polluted evening they shine, if at all, with a less than vigorous light. I stand on the balcony, smoking. All traces of the day's deliria having subsided from the roads beneath me. Like a painted mime faces linger in doorways and in shop windows, each one having pursued his or her "separate interest and pleasure." Each one reluctant to go home. The faces of a city that has died, that has been reborn and has died again. In its canals the waters, still, forgetful and habitual. Dark as the ink of any actuary or obituary. The great warehouses gone. Docks and schools turned into luxury apartments—still vacant. The wind rattles through deserted goods yards at dawn. The bodies of dead soldiers returning. Rumours of another war. Of borders sealed and of people fleeing. No love amongst the populace of a common good at home. Even less of it for those abroad; exploited, murdered or pauperised by those we elected. In cemeteries of de-consecrated churches, in parks, on wayside verges, autumn encamps. Blood red coppices emblazon air. Days shorten. Mist wraps viaducts and bridges. I lean on the balcony, dreaming. Sound of an oratorio through an apartment's broken window. A solitary drunk walks down the side of the road, unseeing. No one pays him any attention. In

51

the canals the waters have begun to harden. Harden around this present. Present which perpetually returns. With a yesterday and a tomorrow; in an unbroken circuit. Taking its place amidst all time's other inventions and appearances. Here, on these roads which no longer vibrate to the triumphal return of armies, it waits, like a foul shadow between the houses, trying to extinguish itself. Enveloping us, too, in its disguises. Seeking, like the stale Ithaka in our bones, a home. Which we, through the grace of our fictions of memory and experience, always provide for it. An exhausted destination. Standing at the door, beckoning us to follow. And we comply. Turning back again to the contaminated moment; of an evening plundered by love or hate. The grey gestation of the day to come, much like the one before. So it was, though they did not know it, when they set out. Dead men singing on the current. Cadavers, not angels, for burying. Men whose narratives would never be completed. Completion requiring surrender. Surrender to what was beyond them. Not suffering—for surfeit of profit or passion. As they left they heard a song above the osier-beds. Fiercely compressed as if it desired never to be repeated. 'Acrocephalus palustris', marsh warbler, singing in a voice reconstituted from all its migrations; each syllable, each phrase, a locus. Singing a song reinscribing in itself the songs of many others. Stumbling through ruined villages at dusk, half full of vermin, they imagined they still heard it. Through fields of unharvested wheat. Presiding at baptisms in remote mountain gorges. Whilst climbing paths treading wild garlic and jasmine into the dust, the sea behind them, before them a fragile carapace of snow and ice—cerement of crystal. No looking back. Whilst scrambling over dry river courses, then down amid arid plains welcomed by horse traders and hunters—for a lame piebald with a downcast look which moved them they bartered a silver fork—through landscapes without cities, without boundaries. Into those immensities of unnavigated, and unrecorded, space and light.

"[June 21st 1571] A long strand broke upon us, suddenly, out of the sea mist and it was as if in that perfect parabola of sand and foam, that gently sluiced—O sempiternal referent!—light, the accumulated rime of all those years sea-wandering was lifted from our eyes. Here, we thought, amidst sweet solaceful scents wafted offshore from some ripe and verdant interior, is the beginning of that world of limitless possibility we had imagined. Day after day, year after year, watching the horizon for sign of some such land, our very selves poured on ahead into the distance, our minds nurtured on the prospect of the destruction of all boundaries. The Absolute, in a form, we veritably believed, of some demiurge or afflatus, beckoned. Only our ever sanguine and sceptical Doctor, Garcia de Aguiar, cautioned us that we might well be pursuing nothing more than residual effects of repeated calentures, or of insufflation of the nerves brought on by too much confinement. 'That unconstrained condition which you seek, too, is not natural. And', he added as an aside, I suspect, upon all our 'continual exploring . . . the whole person is never completely anywhere'"

.....

"[December 12th 1571] On the night air were the odours of burnt meats and the sounds of far off dancing and music. In life, according to our good Doctor, whose discourse inherits the complexion of the Philosopher, one is either moving away from something or someone, there is either a leave taking, or one is moving towards them in impending arrival. Attraction or repulsion, terror or joy, we move, within ourselves, always between opposed or different states and emotions—our being never exclusively engaged within either. Arriving, we are also departing, departing, we are also arriving, and in this slow sad music in which all our lives are conducted there are only impure journeys, imperfect divagations, towards a union which always eludes us. So, as the horse traders settled down with us outside the walls of the city of the ancient kingdom, their mallets pounding tent pegs into hard earth, as dark lanterns swayed in the breeze and braziers of spluttering coals glowed red in the dusk, we were informed that though we had arrived at our destination there was, the good Doctor reiterated (by which some of us were much disquieted), no cause for celebration."

[Translated from Fernão Eannes Azurara's *Jornais*]

Beneath me, on the street, a faint burnishing light. Late November. Cold gleam upon the window. Words from a meeting, past remembering. From another landscape, perhaps, another life. Voice lost in the endless excursus of its re-working. Impersonated persona of another November. Gulls, blown from the headland by the sea wind. White underparts gleaming, incandescent against sky. I listen to their cries above dull accents from the street below. Axles grind the air. In the outer precincts of this paradisio all postal deliveries have been suspended. All postal codes, it is rumoured—rumours, wildly abound—will be abolished. Will they then, I wonder, revert to the Creatrix, to the O of an absence greater than their sum? Our dull sublunary language be superseded, perhaps, all the seas rising around us, by the ethereal music of birds? A gust of wind, thick with the smell of saw-mills and crude oil from refineries, fills the balcony. Under the passing darkness of a squall newspapers and litter are lifted and threshed down emptying streets. Close by a dog howls from a vacant lot. A broken latch bangs on the security gate of a boarded-up beauty parlour. Above the increasing tumult I imagine I catch, for a brief moment, a shard of frenetic song; Acrocephalus palustris, wringing its repertoire of motifs above the osier-beds. Beds where pill-boxes still stand, crumbling on jetties. Where once, damp days among the fens, they waited: time, monotonous and cruel. A continent on fire, a people burning. "Minds bent on a debauchery of destruction . . . a boisterous joy." Windows blacked out. Beyond the saltings dark breakers overwhelmed.

II

"On acacia shaded Station Road not far west of the island capital's main railway station, in a twenty five square feet gravelled enclosure consisting of two wooden benches and on three sides a lichened brick wall backing onto the loading yard of the United Foreign Timber Exporters Company, a minor oddity of this newly independent republic can be found. Here, disproportionate to its surroundings, a statue of Lower Uiper's last Governor General stands—long since shipped from the mainland capital where its presence was deemed 'inappropriate'. Its upkeep now funded by his country's consulate. Towering over a high plinth, regally poised, his hand is outstretched upon a globe. He seems, however, to command within such an inauspicious setting—nothing. An old man with drooping moustaches who arrives with a ladder and brush, with cloths and a bucket to asperge him, can be heard twice a week wheezing rhythmically and asthmatically within his shadow."

.....

"The extreme southern coastal strip from the city of Kasgar is very narrow, hemmed against sea by hills from the east. This part of the coastal region of Lower Uiper is fragmented by deltas. As one proceeds further south the strip widens, the road moving further inland, and one passes through the village of Oka. A poor village of weavers this village was recently badly damaged by mud slips and floods. According to survivors the disaster was preceded by five days of torrential and uninterrupted rain. First there was a slippage of earth and roots, then a large boulder, followed by a whole mountain side. In the illegally logged valley in which Oka nestles, once home to the songs of all kinds of birds, many of the inhabitants died—drowned or immured. On a bare ridge, where the tree line once was, hot wrecking wind and rains broke. Lower down the wind and rain left, the survivors said, a dark mortuary of mud that quickly hardened. The editorial of one leading newspaper later claimed there was 'no foothold on that steep entangled slope of grief for anything but profit.'"

[From Richard Kroll's *Lower Uiper: a Nation Reborn* (1972)]

III

Container/trailer-loads of trinkets & gadgets for an insatiable populace. Inflamed appetency. Blight of consumption. At intervals along the estuary container ports (there is no shrine without a pilgrimage undertaken) where once there were ferry crossings and fordings for sacred destinations. Through scurvy-grass/sea aster/osier-bed up through dense forests long ago obliterated, paths beaten by pilgrims. Bare feet on the rutted highway—its slipper chapels, shrines, hospitals and pyxides of martyr's water—bruised, lacerated, chastened.

I stand alone on the balcony looking out over the city. At mud banks flickering on the river. At vandalised telephone booths and bus shelters. At the many disguises time assumes. Listening, in the noise of each successive moment, arising and departing before me, for the sound of things long dead, and to come. I seem to remember, in another place and another time, a face that is familiar, and wonder, unable to identify it, if it is my first faint recollection of my own. Or one of those other multiple variations upon a face which does not exist, which never existed, but which, out of the remembered warmth of a sunlit gaze, another drear November brings forth. A November as distant and obscure as the pier-heads and bus stations buried under shrouds of mist. Or those words which I daily utter to myself but do not remember, which stand behind me like a half open door—inviting, or defying me, by the weight of their absence, to enter. Above the balcony an eider duck ascends, heading north. The osier-beds are silent, empty. The city is filled with the sounds of departure. Only in the low, rancorous calls of its pedestrians does it recognise the sound of that recurring present of which it is composed. That moment of repetition and recuperation, in which it asserts itself. In which all of its endless grey days and suffocating nights are exhaled upon the minds of those it inhabits. Whose destiny it shapes and unfolds. City, set astride the illusion that space and distance do not exist. That time is infinitely malleable and renewable. Upon its bridges, in its arcades, the visitor lingers and thinks they hear, in its wide avenues and in its squares set back from them, a music of perfect intervals, cadence of stone and air, the absolute architecture of their dreams.

.

By their own beliefs they who set out from salt-eaten quays were corrupted. Fuellers of time and all its fevered forms. Engravers of "pathless winds". Upholders of categories and of classes. Within the mangrove. Upon the beach with the waterfall. Beside the Archive of Ethnological Curiosities. Too much diversity, as if each thing began and ended with itself, demanding too much understanding from them. Lost without water on endless northern plains, stumbled upon by itinerant gatherers of horse droppings. Terror subsiding beneath too much joy. Too much joy subsiding beneath what could not contain it. Hard and affable on the tongues of those they overran their syllables, under the whispering leaves of banana plants, finally, settled.

Over the rooftops, dull gleam of the estuary. On the opposite bank on a horizon of low hills, tall stacks darkly etched, the oil refineries stand in a swathe of late evening light. Drifting down the long gilded stream of air in a billowing procession, a massed riot of cloud; an orange, purple, slate-grey conflagration. It seems to move as if in accord with some deep and urgent compulsion. Because it does so at a height, seemingly, barely above that of the refineries, it appears as if the conflagration issues, there being no smoke without fire, from their stacks. As if all the planet's ancient petrified forests are transpiring again upon the air their brief lives. Burning, in that dark oleaginous element to which they had been consigned, with a bright apocalyptic fury; spreading an ominous red glow over the hills beyond the city.

Envoi

Love, this fragment which attracts, sought after in every gaze and sign, this incompleteness which always goes in search of an other, within whose field of gravitation it is ineluctably pulled. Moving in fear of assassination each night from one official residence in the capital to another, only a handful of trusted aides knowing where he slept. Paid informants in many households. The highways, resplendent in summer, lined with elm and locust trees. For millennia all set to a common gauge, width of rut. Along them, through the high plains, the passes, deserts and the islands, through the far prefectures and vassalages, it called; dust darkening its habiliments. Nothing begins, or ends, in itself.

Notes

Page 51, line 16. J.S. Mill, *On Liberty* (paraphrasing Jeremy Bentham).
Page 55, line 21–22. Rabindranath Tagore, *The Modern Age*.
Page 58, line 3–4. Rabindranath Tagore, *Talks in China* (reformulation of Tagore's "Man cannot reach the shrine, if he does not make the pilgrimage.")
Page 61, line 3 *Bhagavad-Gita* (6: line 38) *Translated by Juan Mascaro*

Ekphrasis

Exhibition of the Newly Restored Arezzo Minerva, 2008–9:
bronze statue with marble copies—

*For Michael Field (Katherine Harris Bradley, Edith Emma Cooper,
aunt and niece, lovers)*

A POEM IN TEN PARTS

1 Goddesses arrive suddenly . . .

fully armed [2]
gathered from dismembered bronze
she has just arrived—
bronze-green lilt of the body—
as if she has already just arrived
leaning on the right leg
poised on the high sandal under
a lilting hem on
the verge of the next step

below high-helmeted rippled hair
a scaled breast plate
coiling with snakes
left hand on hip with drapery tight scrolled
and falling
to the undulating hem just settled
where bronze folds settle to the folds of the air

green-bronze undulating
over high strapped sandals
incised with ivy leaves
scrolled round the toes

coiling hair   scaled snakes
rippling folds
drapery lilting
just settling
with the rush of arrival
to the undulating air [1]

[1] What is it to describe? Does the third section need the first two or do
they need it?
[2] Yes. With a shout she leapt from the forehead of Zeus, in armour, axed
out by three determined gods who cut open the head of Zeus. But she is
not fully armed here: the right arm, leaning on its massive lance, is gone.
A ruined socket, disarmed. The lost part.

*how do you read footnotes—all at the end or in medias res, frequently
interrupting the poem? and would it be a different poem if you read them at
the end or each as they are marked? superscripts. and what are these footnotes
for God's sake, the text's unconscious/my id?*

2
the arrival

in dreams

in bronze

in radiance

owl   snake   gorgon casually worn
on her garments incise
unreconciled
wisdom   cruelty
for ancient wrongs
held high
the serpentine helmet
the eyes
where ivory

or bone
would be   empty
sockets where darkness dwells [1]
who endowed
the eyes that turned all eyes to stone

goddess of knowledge [2]

goddess of violence [3]

daughter of rape [4]

[1] 'Bright-eyed', the poets called her. Those orbital cavities without stone or
   bone now—could they be visionary, or are they just empty?
[2] Wisdom   what did she know? Mucked about by myth.
[3] Minerva created the Medusa's violence by violence. For violating the
   shrine of Minerva by having sex there Medusa's hair became lethal and
   she turned onlookers to stone with her snaky locks. But the seducing
   God Poseidon escaped quite free. Why? Why punish her and let him
   go? Minerva was self-birthed in a manner of speaking, a virgin warrior
   goddess whose shrine to woman was abused. Medusa, lapsing from the
   love of women, should have known better. Poseidon could not have—ig-
   norant jerk.
[4] Zeus violated Metis, thought better of it, gulped down his pregnant lov-
   er. That's how Minerva was born from the god's body. On Zeus and rape
   see Yeats, 'Leda and the Swan': did the great poet's portentous lyricism
   talk nonsense about knowledge and power? How could Leda have 'put
   on' these attributes—like clothes?

or are they, these footnotes, just the sprawling bits that should be tidied away?
The poem's pre- and post- thinking not the poem?

3
standing
in the eternal present tense
of statuary
in a dim gallery
while marble copies of herself [1]

repeat their marble-silent gestures
obey the gerund's necessity
remaking bronze in the present participle of stone [2]

[1] But what is a copy?
[2] Copies in stone as if Medusa had been there. Medusa, endowed with the
    gift of murderous phallic stone, Minerva, all bronze, that pliant alloy, so
    full of sweetness and savagery.

*the problem is a poem breeds commentaries and commentaries on those, an
arachne web of commentary where to stop*

4
her body parts
'found by accident in 1542 near San Lorenzo'
a severed head   a torso
shattered folds and feet
dragged from a well
'taken by Cosimo di Medici to Florence'
whose aesthetic greed
for art's disjecta membra
left the missing right arm amputated in Arezzo [1]
buried somewhere   laved in water
crushed by blocks of stone
two thousand years ago
fallen from a high Etruscan palazzo

[1] Fully armed and disfigured.

*See Adorno on lyric, no poem can stop the questions it asks. Mucked about by
myth and then by the Medicis*

5 & 6 Ekphrasis in Restauro: the catalogue [1]

1542 Cosimo patched her
Francesco Carradori 1785 fixed her
an arm of coloured plaster

at last released
the ancient lyrical figure
by digital image   Xray   scan   computer
freed from history's data
'the strata of successive additions'
into its own past

a grand neo-classical prosthetic gesture
in the antique manner
restored her commanding figure

the removal:
'of the heavy right arm'
'of the mannered gesture of neo-classical rhetoric'
'of the worm-eaten core'
'of the rigid tectonic overlay'
restored:
the head—'a gentle rotation to the right'
the arm—'the absence of the missing right arm'

amended the posture
of head and shoulder
'by thrusting a wooden core into the bronze centre'

the figure—its supple curves
the lyrical body 'whose natural equilibrium
now restored' curves to the play of
flowing folds
green-bronze 'image of youthful freshness
and elegance'
lips slightly apart   full lips 'carnosa'

upright imperial matron and daughter
antiqued by fire [2]

goddess and innamorata
'l'ultimo restauro'
the arrival
of the lover [3]

[1]   This is a layered poem, like the historical layers of restoration, and
      effectively three poems. You can read it as two separate poems in
      sequence or, thirdly, as it is set out above where parts of each poem
      alternate.
[2]   I don't get it quite: the eighteenth century modernised the goddess by
      imagining how the Imperial Romans copied an ancient Greek original
      and restored her to renaissance grandeur.
[3]   This time they made her old again and restored her youth by subtracting
      the burdensome right arm and non-intrinsic surface layers. Restoration
      means taking away now. First time round maternal, virginal, now
      'elegante', sexy. The catalogue keeps wanting to say but can't quite that
      her bottom's neat, exposed by the restorers' feat, fit for a lascivious god.
      Goddess of war, goddess of wisdom, dea, where are you? what happened
      to you?

*they were so certain, Michael Field, of their lyrical note, those lovers,
innamorata, who travelled the art galleries of Europe, seeking out the
strangeness of women in paint, subsequently writing ekphrastic poems from
photographs. Is an ekphrastic poem a restoration?*

7 The Makers B C

released from the final casting
taken away
anima di terra
a core of clay
moulded with beeswax
melted by molten bronze
poured between wax and casing
how many workers
did her body take
in the brute labour of art
made in three pieces

set in folds of
negative space
dream and passion
soul of clay
anima di terra [1]

[1] No room for irony here

*anima di terra, the soul of earth, the soul of clay at the statue's core. no core
poem?*

8 Dating

they made a mistake
she's not from the era
of Imperial Rome
each copper eyelash
each small laminated repair
the chiselled hair
the lips carnosa
each square headed nail
belongs to the late Hellenic period
300 BC
younger than they thought, or older [1]

[14] Dream and passion. Her eight-year repair called up state subsidy
and private funding (banks); the Medici wealth supported the first
restoration. And whose was the immense investment in the passion and
the dream 300 BC, to bring her into being, to make her arrive today, to
create the goddess's arrival, fully armed?

*I know a thought can break hearts in a poem as images do but now how to
how to NOW write lyric in a printed voice*

9 Copies
'un variante al tipo Vescovali cosi da risultare un vero e proprio unicum.' Catalogue

black-green bronze
by herself
alone

among fractured effigies
in carven pallor
and cumbrous marble folds
Vescovali copies in
maimed stone
a splintered torso
weighted with drapery
a head thrown back
whose marble reverie
slow deposits of time
combine to blanche and pit into
petrified swathes of stone [1]

marmor marmor
is there a murmur
to silence? to these supplications
of muteness   gestures that
implore and yet withhold
in reveries of stone?
silence murmurs
have you not forgotten
how you made Medusa?
have you not forgotten
Arachne caught in her own
toils? copies of copies
Benevento Nikopolis Trieste Tivoli
redouble that ancient history

green-black bronze
archetype and original

secondary marble forms
repeat the poised right foot
swathed left arm
the lost arm
fluted hem and helmet
the arrival

and yet and yet
black-green bronze
unicum and variation
who is the first one?
does it matter?—
doubled at the Hermitage
plagiarised at Hadrian's Villa [2]
carved from time and silence
where is the first one
sculpted in marble
that re-members only when it can forget? [3]

[1] No synonyms for stone. There are kinds of stone, granite and marble, and
     sizes, pebbles and boulders. But the irreducible word stone is stone.
[2] the Villa at Tivoli / where a strip of rectangular water / brims with time /
     where white statuary contemplates itself / steeped, oscillating in water in
     an imperceptible breeze / melting . . .
[3] nothing beside remains / those are the pearls that were his eyes / shattered
     visage / lone and level sands that stretch [3a] / foster child of silence and slow
     time / smooth as monumental alabaster / keep a marble or a bronze repose /
     made in bronze for me . . .
[3a] Shelley's Ozymandias sonnet of shattered visage on the internet calls up
     ads for stone crushing machines and remedies for stretch marks.

*the first one—as if it mattered . . . must lyric be pastiche unless it is
commentary?*

10 The children's first sight

and O ecco   and O
there she is
with marble attendants
in the surprise of the arrival
bronze green head high

run and have a look children
at the bronze Minerva
they point
they show one another
even though they all know
each of them is looking
and   O   ecco
show
the toddler reels like a nautical putto
with unstaunched nose
pointing
the girl twirls pointing
the little boy stands still pointing
not turned to stone
they run to a plinth
and swing their feet
and the adults gasp in case they break something [1] Ecco O   and
but [2]

[1] 'as soon as you see something beautiful there is that overwhelming need
   to show it to someone else . . .'
[2] yes, but see above

*I was thinking of Blake's children—she drew a line across the painting and
said I have had my vision—surely not. See above, commentaries
a perfectly good lyric poem torn to pieces*

liminal
(*for dancer Tim Rubidge*)

always
this rocks cumulative rotations

wind drag across bones
tongue becomes fight

the mirror azure
to depths undreamt

unarmed by sun
fist of light tightens

time brittles
with each slow breath

amplify light
bird without roots

a flightless tree
fight and upside

and concrete pages
encourage tears

bloody page spill
lives unread

whose out of step?
turn the book around
feather necessity, flesh
being flesh is torn or worn

at dusk and dust recall
lips skipped in stutter-rhyme
this sweet day, between yourself
and child-song pures

*

outreaching to the broken last, trying to? not so much bridge as
milky-span, toe the line, keep within channels, don't jerky-dance
some magenta-bleed, eyes glide from hand, try some slammer, for
crying out. winged, but then who is? and who is lidless sweat, ever
kneeling, supplication in deep-sunk inhibiting machine

*

light swelters
swells in gesture
jester you
apply match
urging shelter
in airs rare shell
oxygen unfurling
kindling tricks
and again
trip/ripped
ripe flailings
back slam
coincidencing
the spilt up
rouged flight
necessary
as splitting light
pained air lines

reverb blooding
extraordinaire
this arabesques
inked in stutter
mining somewhere
around dawn

spark eyes fruit lung
from tree of body
no sudden gusts
giddying toward
unusual shoulderings
destroy hard data
write vast surfaces
stare unlocked
saffron wide
border is
borders are
wingfold chained
edges of chaos
fist years, flux us
lung ecstatic
grasp at skybreath
your winged tang
on differing tracks

Black Leaves

At dusk, rain begins.
A black bird flies into black leaves.
Rain enters the dry dirt.

I step on an ant.

Last night I could not sleep,
Something buzzed just under my skin.

Today a dragonfly lit on my arm.
Its wings were humming.

Startled, I brushed it off.
The wind blew it back into my face.

Last night I could not sleep.
Something buzzed just under my skin.

The black leaves of the tree are raining.
The black bird has disappeared into rain.

The ant is gone.

Buzzing is the same as humming.
I have no wings.

Green at morning, black at night—
Where are those leaves now?

The ant is in the dirt.
The dirt grows black with rain.
I cannot sleep in this tree.

Recycling Starlight

Is this your destination—the ashes
that were you first sinking back
into damp soil, as if Eden were
a holy compost pile, then spiraling,
invisible, out of that mix into
the gaseous fire of a nascent star?

We often spoke of being recycled,
of how our very molecules were
just visiting. We affirmed the old
adage, *Nothing is ever lost*,
as we sat across from one another,
our computer screens flickering on
and off.

This morning, in my new life
without you, the mulch is pungent
in the flowerbed under my window,
the sky gray and promising rain.

And I wonder—as I breathe
in the fertile air rising
from this garden that waits
for the sun to do its work—
if I'm inhaling you.

Simon Perchik

Eight Poems

*

Every love note starts out warm
sent by one hand over another
is pressing down on this snow

making a fire on her grave, covers it
with those songs from the 40s
still trailing smoke, longing for rain

that's not one night alongside another
each falling off as the name
at the end, a pet name, a secret

you would write on a wall
to whiten it, begin again
already winter and bleeding to death.

*

You always wanted to be near ashes
close to shore, kept warm
between two fires and the afternoons

easing around the rocks
you dead go here with
adrift just below the surface

that has no owner
though nothing falls to the bottom
the way even now the rain

smells from smoke and your coffin
looks for another body
—you wanted to be water, run clear

take your bones with you
and after a long loosening
empty them as a go-between

this hole to lean down
and filling it from shells
not yet your mouth and shoulders.

*

From far off though this wall
still grieves, stone over stone
closing from inside as mist

—still sags into each corner
the way mourners come by in twos
binding their dead to the dim light

that covers the Earth with your forehead
—you're lost, sinking in
till you stop as you did before

and again your back breaks open
for air and wings and in your knees
the bones that will go no further

are filled with an immense arch
pressing down on the thin shadow
waiting at home and loosening.

*

At last and the bare wood
half maple, half before morning
though this rag is already wet

caught up in a seedy summer rain
heated on a table not yet mountainside
wobbling, battered by waiting streams

trying to hold on, drink from a surface
sweetened by water —you lower the cup
face down, help it look for dirt

for its fragrance all night closing in
warmer and warmer alongside a dress
shrunk to fit the soft rim

running naked between your teeth
and dead mornings, around and around
squeezing the sleeves till they go black

the way this washcloth stares in the dark
for a sea to break open, by itself
find mud, the small puddle, her arms.

*

You are mourned the way a child
is taught, stacks wooden blocks
letter by letter letting them topple

spread-eagle into the distance
without a place for corners
or grieve stones —first day in class

and already an uncontrollable glee
growing wild, higher and higher
reeling into sunlight and far off hills

—a five year old Earth, forgetful
hidden from falling skies and shadows
end over end looking for a home

in bedrock, hardened by you dead
still standing by as the dirt handful
everywhere just by moving your hands.

*

Without an address your hands
lean across —another crease
making the final correction

though this note still opens out
windblown, fingerprints
everywhere on her lips

on her breasts, on the bed sheet
folded and over, warmed
for its nakedness and side by side

—every word is already lost
and there at the bottom
where little blossoms should grow

there's nothing but silence
and the long line for a stamp
to cling when it leaves your hands

as if even without the flowers
the corners will arrive as evenings
covered with dirt and her forehead.

*

Just died and its rain
is already snow, comforts
the obituary page

with moonlight pieces
slowly circling down
as that star-shaped lullaby

small stones still look for
—it's this morning's
though over your head the deaths

are hidden in silence
begging for water
that doesn't break apart

the way each sky
is hollowed out for another
—you make a sea

for these dead, each name
a boat, sails, the spray
midair and out loud.

PHILIP KUHN

nicods criterion & the paradox of ravens

the black mirror
which is also the obsidian mirror
through which the oracle returns

the black mirror
which is also
the beautiful black stone
by means of which dr john dee
conjured up the spirits

from the *grim-gribbers*
to the black body bags
masking
unfathomable darkness
eructing from the death
that illumines
the secret ferments of the mind

like
the glassy essence of lies
engraved in
memory
marking
ship s caverns
merging sand out of samphire

at first
men were counterfeited in the elements
then confounded
by the singing of the infinite abundance
even before it was hewn
from the cubic stone

but then men stood / outside the regolith of time
with the smell of carrion carried on the wind
&
turning east ward to watch
over the rising sun would demand to know
what songs the sirens sang

now the ancient mariners have set their sails drifting
over / blake s blackmilkwhite ocean
the black milk
drained from their mother s womb

or yet mother love
still stretches across globe & hemisphere
as perfect   as the song bird named
or as bright as the marrow of the intellectual soul
defiled

t was the stench cast
by mazarine raven & miniscule dove
like the vortex in the plenum

oh   exorbitant night
once
you   desired   that our love   should extend over thresholds
but
chance   encounters   endangered *our* son
& so you
banished the remembrance of him

twas
rugged fate shipwrecked
the one thousand and seventeen lives
as if / each soul had become that song bird named
as her passions violated virgil s slick-sorrowed seas /
or drowned in the white flecked sounds

                that drift over
          the ruby wine-merled waters
    or wash over
          stones / that flail & flutter
             whenever waves crush   exegetical heroes
                or
          fling them hard against
                sacramental creeds

from The Book of Isaac

there is the cool consolation where as for me
already putting out voice in distrustful morning,
everyone who fears awakening the minimum doubt
which you read the following shock which it should expect
threatened when being hardships, forfeit bad ribbon
capital punishment of the typewriter where in any case
because of those of camp illegally adjusts the radio
the good deed of the time of tribulation is this
but & which reads post together with us;
it is that it reaches the point where you are conscious for the
          second time;
as for writing by pencil, possibility of camouflage
which is permitted in this way, with the Minsk reconstruction
depending upon me who am removed just under the refuge
of at least interesting darkness where the fresh air breathes

                    *

but as the flesh fell from his face
vertical pride & bone growth
grey beard & sinks the eye fade
lost without sounding & spark
the full immerse attached spring will survive

living water from natural sources or wells
impure event in some time passes & flow

rainwater must still take its ritual effect
long-fingered hands gentle massage of the forehead
as he peers & pore over the mildewy page

dog's ear & total of old absurd histories
collection of utensils for communicating the past
sanctity of each written object

a sacred protracted taste hope in his lip

*

the woodcarving tradition which delivers
at the duration of centuries reached
at a formidable climax in the throne of Solomon
carved in many components by Aaron Chait from Kelmé,
that life, which is transferred in regard to love,
a very sculptural incorporation of architectural elements,
animals & representation in more than 200 dolls
had mounted in the one cut & scholar, to gather on behalf
of the character at court unwise by wise & formidable kings
extended via biblical histories & popular fable;
as for that kind of constitution, the secure view
which the enormous frequency of current scarcity
is not known with history of art divides
with cause becoming as before, impossible

[The earth   open to the sky]
(*The Birds*)

The earth   open to the sky
receives a graceful light.   The ocean shimmers
along the high California cliffs—
in the openness of the American century
the light falls everywhere—
the clean, well-ordered streets,
the curving Pacific highway,
the white cluster of a village nestled
against the bay.

At the edges,
          forces
              that cannot be acknowledged
flock together, gather strength
for a final assault.

People
     schooled
in unremembered pain, observe
in silence the
        portents
            shaping themselves
        in a blank sky.

Here strange mansions ring out with rote singing
& the dead bleed from empty eye-sockets.
But the true horror is the horror of the perfect coiffure.

The world as we wanted it to be signaling
no more. Bird cries & wingflaps

louder than desire. A new chorus
sounds, rising over the land.

Thinking outside of thought.
Water's edge darkens in elegy.
The world to us:
I will dream you.

[Dusk as a pink & vermillion gashed sky]
(*Stroszek*)

Dusk as a pink-&-vermillion-gashed sky—
    the large-scale beauty of it says, learn to die
        & afterwards cars with their headlights on race
            into darkness until
                the flatness of the land swallows them
                    never touching what it is they came for . . .

ALAN WALL

from Endtimes

Part One: Those Tombs in Ephesus

Dionysius insisted there were the tombs of two Johns in Ephesus, and that is true: I am in both of them. I spent some time on Patmos, then came back here finally. Though written in various cellars of persecution, on an insignificant island, my words commanded attention.

If my Greek is wayward and odd
my Aramaic was a wonder to them all, believe me.
That's how I wrote the gospel
which some redactor cast into the other tongue.
The original lost by Clio's copyists.
Now through the window in the rain
the moon is weeping.
Stars are quicksilver spheres on a black silk windingsheet.

Don't believe the Turin shroud—his was black
woven by the Magdalena from the fleece of a panther
through countless Gethsemane nights.
She knew her beloved Lord would lie inside it
shortly.

If it's evidence of chronology you need
read these gospels
each authentically carbon-dated
by our grief. Taste
the acrid stink of desolation's cellar.
Penned in that catacomb each hides inside himself.

My words have resurrected him
as he dictated. My work now's
writing his life, tending his mother.

Never a tear from her
since that day on Golgotha.
Should they fall they'd not be
salt water, but atoms, weapons-grade
plutonium, angry enough to eat the whole of Ephesus
leaving it void and smoking.
She keeps a drawer full of resurrection name-tags.

Revise.
Dead man rising in his rags
to stare incredulous into a saviour's face.
And now they say that in the colosseums
lions feed upon his testament.
(Should *Hegemon* be used, I wonder,
in the passages concerning Pilate?)
Beloved disciple
a man hunted and haunted from Palestine to Patmos
half-insane with emblems, symbols,
eschatological venom.

The world will end one day
he said: never attempt to compute it.
She says almost nothing now.
With the boy at last outside her womb
the end of the world began.
Such a calm here finally
sharing our endings in Ephesus.

This afternoon as I wrote
she spent two hours staring
at a dead sparrow on the windowsill.
An invisible hand will surely
come to revive it.
I place a cup of red wine in her palms

and she looks down
as if at blood.
Who needs reminding of its colour?
She thinks she might have left some trinkets
on the dark side of the moon—
old CDs; an album of photographs—
a young boy learning the rudiments of carpentry
from his earthly father. Her son, she says,
will collect them for her
once he gets back home and picks up his messages.
The journey turned out longer than we'd thought.

(There is a tradition that, after the crucifixion, the disciple John went to Ephesus accompanied by Mary. There they both lived to a great age. An early account held that the author of The Gospel According to John *was one and the same as the author of* Revelation. *This has been disputed for centuries. The texts are so different. But written in different languages, different genres, different times, might they still claim a single author? No one actually knows. In any case, you can't always choose your redactor. History assigns them. One thing we do know: after the original document was written, it has never ceased to be re-written, in accordance with each new generation's millenarian expectations. Apocalyptic visions born at the heart of the Empire.)*

Part Three: Elegiac Days

The emperor always fears assassination.

Domitian my tormentor
spent hours alone each day
spearing flies
with a needle-sharp pen
while my own nib furrowed the parchment
here on Patmos.

Look at him now in his garden.
The seedlings hurrying and swerving around him.
Snowflakes translated to summer.

Always surrounded by priests and priestesses
devotees of one sacred cult or another.
Unchaste vestals he had executed:
Cornelia, Chief-Vestal, buried alive
her lovers clubbed to death
before an avid Roman crowd.
His interest in chastity was not impartial always:
seduced his brother's daughter
who died of the abortion
he forced on her.

Still he valued justice and propriety.
Castration he prohibited then strictly controlled
the price of eunuchs already in the dealers' hands.
His reign full of portents. An eagle (my symbol too)
screeched while embracing his statue at Rome
and a raven perched on the Capitol croaking "All will be well"
but he didn't believe it, preferring "Nevermore".
Took writing seriously, gave poetry readings
in his early years, sending to Alexandria
for volumes missing from his library.
Hermogenes forfeited his life through unfortunate allusions
in a historical opus, while his copyists, slaves, were crucified
for exactitude in transmission.
Like Stalin, an affable host
inviting a Palace steward to his bedroom, sharing dinner,
the luxurious couch. Only thing missing
was the vodka.
Come morning the fellow was crucified.

Suspicion now his element.
His daily exercise-gallery lined with
polished moonstone so he could see
any assassin approaching from behind.
Murdered at last by his friends
with his wife's connivance
as stars had predicted. Minerva told him in a dream
how Jupiter disarmed her.

The blade went in repeatedly as later an ice-axe
would hack through Trotsky's head.
Writing until the very end.

My hand moves over this page
as dawn over Patmos
announces fresh calamities.

My name is John and I am obliged to give witness
to events informed
by history's nightmare, ushering in
the day of judgment—
kingdom come.

I sit here pen in hand
imposing Hebrew forms on Greek constructions
awaiting the knock on the door
in the early hours
sharing such revelation with prophets
already past, and some still to come.

Mandelstam they came for in darkness
who never walked as I did once
along the shores of Galilee
swallowing the sun as though it were
wine in a silver chalice.

JUAN ANTONIO GONZÁLEZ-IGLESIAS

TRANSLATED BY CURTIS BAUER

Question with an Answer That Doesn't Matter

for Christian Law Palacín

A medieval theologist asks
if two angels
can
speak—converse—
without the other angels hearing them.
The answer doesn't matter
but the almost
physical sensation
that beneath these symbolic codes
one can draw an exact
definition of how
poetry can be
transmitted
in book form, and this strange
pleasure
that spiritual things allow
provided
that they are written in lower case.

The Reign of Hadrian

*It's about, above all, a theory of knowledge, of the manner in which
a man steals himself little by little from the ideas of his time which
he rejects.*
> Marguerite Yourcenar [on Zeno],
> Letter to Alain Bosquet, January 1, 1964

The reign of Hadrian
is like the October the Japanese
celebrate. But the nostalgia
I feel from those years isn't a result
of the absence of gods. Nor is it due to
the joyful government of this monarch.
Nor to the Hellenic culture, his trips
or the stability of the borders
of his empire. I recognize
that as my homeland,
as my own time,
because I sense that then I wouldn't have
this feeling of deepening
exile that wakes
in me the age that I have been given,
the anguishing culture
dictated by some who don't love,
the intellectuals
of the middle class, those
who are neither poets nor philosophers,
the cloudy future,
the uncertain situation of my country.

The Love Poem Should Have

You see where you're going on the bus
E.M.T. Madrid

The love poem should have the future
course of the heavens in mind
but also
the vocabulary of the route
and the simple glory of the minute.
It should anticipate the word Albertur
only because it is written on the side
of the night bus that takes you back home.
It should talk about the city outskirts,
accept what it sees for where it goes,
and from our lips become
an ode to lighted cities.
It should have failures in mind,
all of our poverty,
the fear that our love could break against walls.
The love poem should know that we are
equal, and it should also include your name and my name,
in the manner that my name includes yours. This way
I won't say Petrarch doesn't matter to us.
I'll say that he's not enough. Our fire comes from
further away than the end of the world.

If the cypress and rain have the same form,
I don't want to be obscure, or poor in adventure.

Thomas Aquinas Declares That The Devil

—for Francisco Fortuny

Thomas Aquinas declares that the devil
hates hierarchy, because he knows
that order is an ascending scale toward God.
However, Francis
of Assisi—who desired
to follow, naked, the naked God—
declared himself outside any type of hierarchy.
One of the two is a liar. I think it's Thomas Aquinas.

from Triste Tristan

They're still in our heads the good old fellows
let's talk hormones
a monologue of the deaf—
we allow a ration of free sex
down at the ford—
would have to be dumb not to sing
now
that the story's all over the world.

Béroul and Thomas,
of course we've read them,
bring up fornication
in every line—
a chance to embroider:
a tale of love won't always
lead
to sexual reproduction—
terror isn't the last word from heaven
we need the natives
for the lowdown.

Gains prestige
being on top of the queen—
she snaps, hurls insults
can't take it no more—
he, aggressive, comes—

99

two dogs stuck together
their talk
a slew of droppings—
I'll add a fool a dwarf a messenger—
as best I can.

Is nonetheless a cuckold,
par for a horse—
jeers at the one he adored.
his face drenched with rain—
a spectacle with plenty of spies,
enemies of abstract art
forced to pipe down.

International debacle—this job of
the enraged husband—
beware the mangy cur, disgustingly
happy—good for nothing
howling at the merciful sky—
I get lost here, all these memories
and the piles of critical editions.

Stick it to me, your dick,
says Iseut (would you believe it)—
everybody believes it
to the point, precisely, where
God is hard pressed preaching love—
God, would you believe it,

rustling in flowing robes
and complicit—
otherwise how explain it—
they never stop,
he's going to kill her right there under him.

Iseut, black sky between her tits—
makes me hungry— me
who never thought I'd need
to thrown myself on the bread—
this piece of Iseut:
thorax night,
tear at it with my teeth—likewise
smashed dishes
around them—something
makes them lose it.

ÉLISE TURCOTTE   *TRANSLATED BY ANDREA MOORHEAD*

Five Poems

Dream where fear
is queen
as in a painting
where birds strike
the window
before devouring each other

My yard is covered
with a layer
of unknown material

I make the rounds
of the boutique
of evil spells
finding
neither prayer
nor magic formula

*

Children also
are destroyed
there's a fire
behind the barricades
I can imagine
the chapel full
of hands, of sighs
piles of shoes lie unclaimed

abandoned
on the marble floor
war took a picture
of its people
but despair here
has no bond
it's fluid
perfect
like the song
of a shell

*

The tombstones with children's
silhouettes
are the most difficult
to look at
they still carry names
that fly away
at the least breeze
then lie about
in such a lonely place
that I'd like to be imprisoned
there where the void remains

*

The wind doesn't exist anymore
my own movements
are led

by a secret understanding
between forms
between black and white
and the impure colors
occasionally an object drowns
beside me
I can feel
its slowness

*

I cannot understand
you repeated words
burned
hard like mine
fields
you said them
in your reality
overflowing with ideas
but I don't know
I don't know
watching the words
fall one by one
then form
a kind of coil
in the silt

Notes on Contributors

Martin Anderson has been publishing with *Shearsman* since the very first issue. Recent books from Shearsman: *The Hoplite Journals* (2006), *Belonging* (2009), and *The Hoplite Journals XXX–LVIX* (2010).

Isobel Armstrong is Emeritus Professor of English at Birkbeck, University of London, and a Senior Research Fellow of the Institute of English Studies at the University of London. She was featured in the anthology *Infinite Difference* (Shearsman Books, 2010), and in a chapbook, *Desert Collages* (Equipage, 2007). Critical work includes *Victorian Glassworlds: Glass Culture and the Imagination 1830–1880* (OUP, 2008).

Curtis Bauer won the John Ciardi Poetry Prize for his first poetry collection, *Fence Line* (BkMk, 2004), and has been a finalist for the *New Letters* Poetry Prize, The Willis Barnstone Translation Prize, and The *Glimmer Train* Poetry Open. He is the publisher and editor of Q Ave Press Chapbooks and teaches creative writing and translation at Texas Tech.

Sean Burn has 3 full-length collections, most recently *wings are giving out* (Cardigan: Skrev Press, 2009).

Susan Conolly's first collection of poetry, *For the Stranger*, was published by the Dedalus Press in 1993. Her second collection, *Forest Music*, was published by Shearsman Books in 2009. She lives in Drogheda, Ireland.

Ray DiPalma lives in New York City; he is the author of a number of books, most recently *The Ancient Use of Stone: Journals and Daybooks 1998–2008*. (Otis Books, Los Angeles, 2009). His visual works (including artist's books, collages, and prints) have been exhibited in numerous shows in the United States, Europe, Japan and South America, and in a one-person show at the Stempelplatt's Gallery in Amsterdam.

Gareth Durasow has work in *Onedit, Great Works, Spine, Grist and Freak Lung* and *Sunfish*, and a chapbook, *Obelus* (Knives, Forks & Spoons, 2010).

Amy Evans' poetry, art-work and critical writing have been published in *Openned, Jacket* and *The Wolf* respectively. She is completing a PhD on Robert Duncan at King's College London; she was co-editor, with Shamoon Zamir, of *The Unruly Garden: Robert Duncan and Eric Mottram, Letters & Essays* (Peter Lang: 2007).

Juan Antonio González-Iglesias is Professor of Latin Philology at the University of Salamanca, Spain. He has translated Ovid, Horace, Catullus, Stendhal and Sebastiano Grasso. In addition to *Eros es más* (selected by *El Cultural, El Mundo* as Spain's best collection of poetry in 2007), his other collections of poetry include *La hermosura del héroe* (Premio Vicente Núñez, 1993), *Esto es mi cuerpo* (Visor, 1997), *Más hermosura* (CELYA, 2002), *Un ángulo me basta* (Visor, 2002) and *Olímpicas* (El Gaviero Ediciones, 2005).

ANNE GORRICK lives in New York's Hudson Valley. She has two volumes from Shearsman: *Kyotologic* (2008) and *I-Formation, Book 1* (2010).

PENNY HARTER lives in New Jersey, and is the author of a number of books, most recently *The Night Marsh* (WordTech Editions, 2008). Penny and her late husband, Bill Higginson, both featured in early editions of *Shearsman*.

PAOL KEINEG is a Breton poet and dramatist who writes in both Breton and French. He teaches at Duke University in North Carolina and has published almost 20 books, including *Lieux communs* (Gallimard, 1980), *Triste Tristan* (éditions Apogée, 2004), *Les trucs sont démolis* (Le temps qu'il fait/Obsidiane, 2008). In English: *Boudica* (tr. Rosmarie Waldrop. Burning Deck, 1994)

PHILIP KUHN's *at maimonides table* was published by Shearsman in 2009. His co-translations of German poet, Gertrud Kolmar, will also appear from Shearsman. The text here is scission 4 from *how to make radical leaflets*, just published by itinerant press.

JOHN LEVY lives in Tucson, Arizona, where he works as an attorney. He was one of the contributing editors in the first series of Shearsman. He has recently published a prose volume, *A Mind's Cargo Shifting* (First Intensity Press); his last poetry collection was *Oblivion, Tyrants, Crumbs* (2008) from the same publisher.

JOHN MATEER lives in Western Australia, but was born in South Africa. Books include The West (Fremantle Press, 2010), *The Ancient Capital of Images* (Fremantle Arts Centre Press, 2005), and the bilingual volume *Ex-white/Einmal-Weiss: South African Poems* (Klagenfurt: Sisyphus, 2009). Forthcoming is *Southern Barbarians* (Giramondo).

CHRISTOPHER MIDDLETON is one of the UK's finest poets. Carcanet published his *Collected Poems* in 2008, and Shearsman recently published his *Poems 2006–2009*, comprising all the work composed since the *Collected* was assembled. Christopher Middleton's work was featured in the first series of *Shearsman* in 1981–1982.

ANDREA MOORHEAD is editor of *Osiris* and a translator of contemporary Francophone poetry. She publishes in both French and in English. Poems and translations have appeared in journals such as *Abraxas, Great River Review, The Bitter Oleander, Autre Sud, Estuaire, La Traductière,* and *Metamorphoses*. Collections include *From a Grove of Aspen* (University of Salzburg Press), *le vert est fragile*, and *Présence de la terre* (Écrits des Forges). Translations include books by Hélène Dorion, Abderrahmane Djelfaoui and Madeleine Gagnon.

TOBY OLSON divides his time between Philadelphia and North Truro, on Cape Cod. His most recent novel is *Tampico* (University of Texas Press, 2008); his most recent poetry collection is *Darklight* (Shearsman, 2007). Toby Olson's work was featured in the first series of *Shearsman*.

SIMON PERCHIK has been a regular in *Shearsman* since its first days. His first six books were all published by the Elizabeth Press in the 1960s and 1970s, and his collected poems, *Hands Collected 1949–1999*, appeared in 2000 (Pavement Saw Press, 2000; 2nd ed., 2003). Subsequent books include *Touching the Headstone* (Stride, 2000), *Rafts* (Parsifal Press, 2007), *Greatest Hits: 1964–2008* (Pudding House Publications).

PETER ROBINSON is a professor of English and American Literature at the University of Reading. His many books include *The Look of Goodbye* (poetry, Shearsman, 2008), *Spirits of the Stair* (aphorisms, Shearsman, 2009), and a *Selected Poems* from Carcanet Press.

AIDAN SEMMENS lives in Suffolk and is a journalist. His first full-length collection, *A Stone Dog*, appears shortly from Shearsman.

NATHANIEL TARN, poet, essayist, anthropologist, and translator, lives in New Mexico. Most recent books: *Avia* (Shearsman, 2008), *Ins and Outs of the Forest Rivers* (New Directions, 2008), *The Embattled Lyric: Conversations and Essays in Poetics and Anthropology* (Stanford University Press, 2007). His work was published in the first series of *Shearsman* in 1981.

JON THOMPSON a professor of English at North Carolina State University, where he edits *Free Verse: A Journal of Contemporary Poetry & Poetics* and Free Verse Editions. His first collection of poems was *The Book of the Floating World* (Parlor Press, 2007). Shearsman published his collection of essays, *After Paradise*, in 2009.

NATHAN THOMPSON is currently studying for a PhD at the University of Salford. His first collection, *the arboretum towards the beginning*, was published by Shearsman in 2008.

ÉLISE TURCOTTE was born in Sorel, Québec, and has published ten collections of poetry, for which she has received numerous prizes. Her most recent books are *Ce qu'elle voit* (Noroît, 2010), *Piano mélancolique* (Noroît, 2005) and *Sombre ménagerie* (Noroît, 2002). She has also published several books for children, short stories, and three novels.

ROSMARIE WALDROP appeared as both poet and translator in the first series of *Shearsman*. She is the author of a number of books, six of them from New Directions (most recently *Driven to Abstraction*, 2010), and the translator of many more, from both German and French, with her many renderings of Edmond Jabès justly celebrated. With husband Keith, she runs Burning Deck Press, a beacon of light in the darkness for several decades.

ALAN WALL is a professor at the University of Chester. Author of a number of novels, most recently *Sylvie's Riddle* (London: Quartet Books, 2008), his poetry is published by Shearsman: *Gilgamesh* (2008), *Alexander Pope at Twickenham* (2008) and *Doctor Placebo* (2010).

www.ingramcontent.com/pod-product-compliance
Lightning Source LLC
Chambersburg PA
CBHW030958090426
42737CB00007B/582